From Home to Halls:

A Student's Guide to Smooth Relocation and Thriving on Campus

Ann Adams

@Copyright 2024 Ann Adams - All rights reserved

The characters and events portrayed in this book are fictitious. Any similarity to real persons, living or dead, is coincidental and not intended by the author.

No part of this book may be reproduced, or stored in a retrieval system, or transmitted in any form or by any means, electronic, mechanical, photocopying, recording, or otherwise, without express written permission of the publisher.

The views expressed in this book are those of the author and do not necessarily reflect the views of the publisher. The mention of specific companies or certain products does not constitute an endorsement by the author or publisher.

The information in this book is provided "as is" and without warranties of any kind, either express or implied. To the fullest extent permissible pursuant to applicable law, the author and publisher disclaim all warranties, express or implied, including, but not limited to, implied warranties of merchantability and fitness for a particular purpose. The author and publisher do not warrant that the contents of this book are error-free.

All trademarks and registered trademarks appearing in this book are the property of their respective owners.

By using this book, the reader agrees to the terms and conditions stated above. If you do not agree with these terms and conditions, please do not use this book.

Cover design by: Ann Adams

Table of Contents

Introduction: The Thrill and Trepidation of New Beginnings 8

Chapter 1: Embracing the Journey: From Acceptance to Action 10

    1.1 Riding the Wave of Acceptance: From Celebration to Strategy 11

    1.2 Assembling Your Dream Team: Building a Support System 13

    1.3 Budgeting Like a Boss: Mastering the Financial Factor 15

    1.4 Dorm Sweet Dorm: Navigating Housing Options 16

    1.5 The Art of Letting Go: Decluttering and Downsizing 18

Chapter 2: Mastering the Move: Logistics and Practicalities 20

    2.1 Planes, Trains, and Automobiles: Transportation and Logistics 21

    2.2 Packing Prowess: From Clothes to Coffee Makers .. 22

    2.3 The Big Day: Conquering Move-In Day 24

    2.4 Dorm Room Essentials and Hacks: From Functional to Fabulous 25

    2.5 Safety and Security: Protecting Your Personal Haven 27

Chapter 3: Building Your Nest: Creating a Home Away from Home 29

    3.1 Personalizing Your Space: From Blank Canvas to Cozy Haven 30

    3.2 Roommate Harmony: Building a Respectful and Supportive Cohabitation 31

3.3 Conquering Chaos: Organization and Time Management Strategies 33

3.4 Finding Your Tribe: Building a Community on Campus 34

3.5 From Dependent to Independent: Fostering Responsibility and Self-Reliance 35

Chapter 4: Academic Success: Strategies for Thriving in College 38

4.1 Navigating the Academic Landscape: Understanding the System 39

4.2 Cracking the Study Code: Mastering the Art of Learning 40

4.3 Professors as Allies: Building Relationships for Success 42

4.4 Balancing Act: Juggling Academics and Social Life 43

4.5 Overcoming Academic Hurdles: Bouncing Back from Setbacks 45

Chapter 5: Wellness and Self-Care: Prioritizing Your Well-being 47

5.1 Fueling Your Body and Mind: Maintaining Physical Health 48

5.2 Taming the Mental Monsters: Managing Stress and Anxiety 49

5.3 Building Healthy Relationships: Fostering Connection and Support 51

5.4 Home Is Where the Heart Is: Staying Connected with Loved Ones 52

5.5 Cultivating Optimism: The Power of a Positive Mindset 54

Chapter 6: Navigating Social Life and Campus Culture 56

6.1 Decoding the Social Scene: Exploring Campus Culture 57

6.2 From Classmates to Companions: Making Friends and Building Connections 58

    6.3 Navigating the Dating Game: Relationships in the College Realm...59

    6.4 Partying Smart: Balancing Fun with Responsibility 62

    6.5 Embracing Diversity and Inclusion: Building a Welcoming Community...64

Chapter 7: Beyond the Campus: Exploring Your Surroundings 67

    7.1 Discovering Hidden Gems: Exploring the Local Community..68

    7.2 Navigating the Urban Jungle: Transportation and Getting Around 69

    7.3 Weekend Wanderlust: Planning Adventures and Exploring Beyond 71

    7.4 Financial Independence: Budgeting Beyond the Campus Bubble...72

    7.5 Building a Future: Exploring Career Options and Opportunities 74

Conclusion:...76

Embracing the Journey, Shaping Your Future 76

References: 79

Introduction: The Thrill and Trepidation of New Beginnings

"The magic thing about home is that it feels good to leave, and it feels even better to come back." - Wendy Wunder

The fat envelope arrives, or perhaps it's a jubilant email notification. Your heart races as you tear it open, or click to read the news. "Congratulations!" it proclaims, and suddenly your future explodes with possibility. You're going to college! Elation, excitement, and maybe a touch of disbelief wash over you. This is the moment you've dreamt of, worked towards, and now it's finally here. Yet, amidst the thrill, a flutter of anxiety takes flight. Leaving the comfort of home, navigating a new environment, and embracing the unknown – it's a whirlwind of emotions.

Take a deep breath. This is where your adventure truly begins.

"From Home to Halls" is your roadmap to not just surviving, but thriving as you embark on this exciting chapter. We'll unpack the practicalities of moving, from decluttering your belongings to mastering dorm room organization. But this guide goes beyond boxes and checklists. We'll delve into the heart of the college experience, exploring how to build a sense of belonging, cultivate meaningful relationships, and conquer the academic challenges that lie ahead.

We'll equip you with tools to navigate the social scene, prioritize your well-being, and even explore the world beyond campus. This is your journey to independence, self-discovery, and ultimately, success.

So, whether you're feeling a mix of exhilaration and apprehension, or simply eager to dive into this new chapter, consider this book your companion. Let's turn those pre-college jitters into a launchpad for an unforgettable experience. Welcome to the exciting world of college life – are you ready to make it your own?

Chapter 1: Embracing the Journey: From Acceptance to Action

"The journey of a thousand miles begins with a single step." - Lao Tzu

That first step, the one that propels you from high school senior to college freshman, is often fueled by a potent mix of exhilaration and apprehension. The acceptance letter is a tangible symbol of your achievements, a gateway to new opportunities and experiences. Yet, the path forward might seem shrouded in a mist of unknowns.

This chapter is your compass, guiding you through the initial whirlwind of emotions and helping you transform nervous anticipation into productive action. We'll map out the first steps on your college journey, from celebrating your acceptance to tackling pre-move tasks with newfound clarity and confidence. You'll learn how to build a support system, manage the financial aspects of this transition, and navigate the exciting world of housing options.

Get ready to embrace the journey – it's time to turn your college dreams into reality.

1.1 Riding the Wave of Acceptance: From Celebration to Strategy

"The future belongs to those who believe in the beauty of their dreams." - Eleanor Roosevelt

Let's face it, that acceptance letter isn't just a piece of paper – it's a golden ticket to a world brimming with possibility. It's the culmination of countless hours spent hunched over textbooks, fueled by caffeine and sheer determination. It's the payoff for every late-night study session and early morning alarm. So go ahead, do your victory dance, shout it from the rooftops, and let the wave of euphoria carry you away! You've earned this moment of pure, unadulterated joy.

But as the initial excitement settles, a new question arises: "What's next?" This is where the true adventure begins, future scholar. It's time to harness that exhilaration and transform it into a roadmap for success. We're not talking about boring to-do lists and rigid schedules, but rather a strategic approach to navigating this exciting transition.

First things first, let's celebrate!

Take a moment to appreciate the magnitude of your accomplishment. Reflect on the hurdles you've cleared and the dedication you've poured into reaching this milestone. This is a moment to bask in the glow of your achievements and acknowledge the incredible individual you've become. Savor the sweetness of success – you deserve it!

Next, share the joy!

Gather your family and friends, those who have cheered you on and offered unwavering support throughout your journey. Their pride and excitement will amplify your own, creating a powerful network of encouragement as you embark on this new chapter. Let them share in your happiness and build a foundation of support that will bolster you throughout your college experience.

And remember, it's okay to feel overwhelmed.

Excitement, anticipation, maybe even a touch of nervousness – it's all part of the emotional rollercoaster that comes with such a significant life change. Embrace the full spectrum of your emotions and don't be afraid to express them. Talk to someone you trust about your hopes and anxieties, and remember, you're not alone in this journey. Thousands of students across the country are experiencing the same mix of emotions, embarking on their own unique college adventures.

With a celebratory spirit and a supportive network, you're ready to transform those "what now?" anxieties into a clear vision for your future.

Let's dive into the first steps of this exciting transition and turn your college dreams into a concrete plan.

1.2 Assembling Your Dream Team: Building a Support System

College is an exciting adventure, but let's be real, it can also feel like navigating a jungle without a map. That's where your support system comes in – your very own team of cheerleaders, advisors, and confidants who will be there for you through thick and thin. Building a strong support network is crucial for a smooth transition and a successful college experience.

Think of it like assembling your own superhero squad, each member equipped with unique skills and knowledge to guide and support you.

First up, connect with your fellow adventurers!

Social media and online forums are fantastic tools for connecting with future classmates. Search for your college's official pages and student groups – you'll find a wealth of information and a community of excited individuals embarking on the same journey. Strike up conversations, ask questions, and start building friendships even before you set foot on campus. Remember, these connections could blossom into lifelong friendships or even future study buddies.

Next, seek wisdom from those who've walked the path before you.

Reach out to current students or alumni of your college. They've been in your shoes and can offer invaluable insights into campus life, academic expectations, and even the best places to grab a late-night snack. Many colleges have mentorship programs or online platforms where you can connect with current students. Don't hesitate to ask questions and soak up their wisdom – they're a treasure trove of information and support.

And of course, your family and friends are your OG support crew.

Open and honest communication with your loved ones is essential during this transition. Share your anxieties and excitement, seek their advice, and let them know how they can best support you. Whether it's a listening ear, a helping hand with packing, or simply a reassuring hug, their presence will be a source of comfort and strength as you navigate this new chapter.

Remember, you don't have to go it alone. By building a strong support system, you'll have a team of champions by your side, cheering you on and helping you navigate the exciting, and sometimes challenging, world of college life.

1.3 Budgeting Like a Boss: Mastering the Financial Factor

College is an investment in your future, but let's be honest, it can also feel like a crash course in personal finance. From tuition fees to textbooks to those tempting late-night pizza runs, the costs can quickly add up. But fear not, future financial wizard, this is your chance to take control and master the art of budgeting.

Think of it as a game, where you're the savvy player strategically managing your resources to achieve victory – aka a fulfilling and financially responsible college experience.

First, let's create a realistic budget.

Grab a notebook, open a spreadsheet, or download a budgeting app – whatever floats your financial boat. Start by listing all your anticipated expenses: tuition, housing, meals, textbooks, transportation, and of course, a little fun money. Be honest with yourself and factor in those spontaneous purchases and weekend adventures.

Next, explore your funding options.

Scholarships, grants, financial aid, and work-study programs are your allies in this financial quest. Research scholarship opportunities that align with your academic achievements, interests, or background. Fill out the FAFSA (Free Application for Federal Student Aid) to determine your eligibility for government aid and explore work-study programs offered by your college. Remember, every dollar counts!

Finally, it's time to level up your money management skills.

College is a stepping stone to independence, and that includes financial independence. Learn the basics of budgeting, saving, and responsible credit card use. Explore tools and apps that can help you track your spending, set financial goals, and avoid those impulse purchases that can derail your budget.

Remember, financial responsibility isn't about deprivation, it's about making informed choices and ensuring your money is working for you. By taking control of your finances, you'll not only conquer college costs but also build a solid foundation for a successful financial future.

1.4 Dorm Sweet Dorm: Navigating Housing Options

Ah, the dorm room – your home away from home, your personal haven within the bustling campus ecosystem. It's where late-night study sessions turn into impromptu dance parties, where instant ramen becomes a gourmet meal, and where lifelong friendships are forged. But before you start picturing perfectly curated Instagram-worthy décor, let's explore the exciting world of college housing options.

Think of it like choosing your own adventure, each housing option offering a unique experience and catering to different preferences and needs.

First, understand the lay of the land.

Most colleges offer a variety of housing options, from traditional dorm rooms to suite-style living to apartment complexes. Research the different types of housing available on your campus, paying attention to amenities, floor plans, and location. Consider factors like whether you prefer a shared or private room, a communal bathroom or an en-suite, and proximity to academic buildings or social hubs.

Next, delve into the details.

Research dorm amenities, rules, and regulations. Is there a communal kitchen? Laundry facilities on each floor? What are the guest policies? Understanding the ins and outs of dorm life will help you make an informed decision and ensure a smooth transition.

Finally, consider the roommate factor.

Living with a roommate can be an enriching experience, offering companionship, support, and endless late-night conversations. However, compatibility is key. If possible, connect with potential roommates before move-in day to discuss living habits, study preferences, and expectations for shared space.

Remember, your dorm room is more than just a place to sleep – it's your home base, your sanctuary within the vibrant college community. By carefully considering your housing options and planning accordingly, you'll create a comfortable and inspiring space to learn, grow, and make unforgettable memories.

1.5 The Art of Letting Go: Decluttering and Downsizing

Let's face it, your childhood bedroom probably resembles a museum dedicated to your life thus far – overflowing with clothes you haven't worn since middle school, trophies from long-forgotten victories, and enough stuffed animals to start your own zoo. But as you embark on your college adventure, it's time to channel your inner Marie Kondo and embrace the art of letting go.

Think of it as a liberating experience, shedding the weight of accumulated belongings and creating space for new experiences and memories.

First, take inventory.

Sort through your belongings and ruthlessly evaluate what sparks joy (thanks, Marie!) and what simply takes up space. Be honest with yourself – do you really need that collection of novelty socks or those dusty trophies from elementary school? Categorize your items into piles: keep, donate, sell, or toss.

Next, embrace the power of organization.

Invest in packing supplies – boxes, bins, labels – and create a system for organizing your belongings. Pack essentials separately for easy access on move-in day. Remember, dorm rooms are notorious for their lack of storage space, so prioritize multi-functional furniture and space-saving solutions.

Finally, consider the sentimental stuff.

There will undoubtedly be items with sentimental value that you can't bear to part with. Instead of cramming them into your already overflowing suitcase, consider creating a memory box to store at home or taking photos of cherished items to bring with you.

Remember, decluttering is not just about getting rid of stuff – it's about creating space for new beginnings. By letting go of the old, you open yourself up to the exciting possibilities that college life has to offer. So, embrace the minimalist mindset, pack light, and embark on your college journey with a sense of freedom and clarity.

Chapter 2: Mastering the Move: Logistics and Practicalities

"A journey is best measured in friends, rather than miles." - Tim Cahill

The excitement is building, the packing boxes are piling up, and your college adventure is just around the corner. But before you can dive headfirst into dorm life and campus shenanigans, there's the little matter of actually getting there. Moving to college is a logistical dance, a carefully choreographed sequence of packing, planning, and perhaps a few moments of controlled chaos.

But fear not, future logistical master, this chapter is your ultimate guide to navigating the move with grace and efficiency. We'll delve into the nitty-gritty of transportation options, packing strategies, and conquering move-in day like a seasoned pro.

Get ready to transform those moving day jitters into a seamless transition, because with a little planning and preparation, you'll be settling into your dorm room and embracing college life before you know it.

2.1 Planes, Trains, and Automobiles: Transportation and Logistics

So you've conquered the decluttering challenge and your belongings are neatly packed (or at least contained within a reasonable number of boxes). Now comes the exciting part: actually getting yourself and your stuff to college! Whether you're moving across town or across the country, there are a multitude of transportation options to consider.

Think of it as choosing your own adventure, each mode of transport offering a unique blend of convenience, cost-effectiveness, and maybe even a scenic road trip playlist.

First, weigh your options.

Are you planning to fly solo, embark on a family road trip, or entrust your belongings to a professional moving service? Each option comes with its own set of pros and cons. Flying might be the quickest option, especially for long distances, but consider luggage restrictions and potential costs. Driving offers flexibility and the opportunity for a memorable road trip, but factor in gas expenses, potential tolls, and the stamina required for a long drive. Moving services can alleviate the stress of transporting bulky items, but they come at a premium price.

Next, map out your route.

If you're driving, plan your itinerary in advance. Research rest stops, gas stations, and potential overnight accommodations. Consider traffic patterns and weather conditions, and be sure to share your route with family and friends for safety purposes.

Finally, don't forget the essentials.

Ensure you have all necessary documents for travel, including your driver's license, car insurance information, and any required student identification. If flying, confirm baggage allowances and any restrictions on items you can bring. Pack a travel essentials bag with necessities like medications, chargers, and a change of clothes in case of unexpected delays.

Remember, the journey to college is just as important as the destination. By choosing the right transportation method and planning your route carefully, you'll arrive on campus feeling refreshed, excited, and ready to embark on your college adventure.

2.2 Packing Prowess: From Clothes to Coffee Makers

Ah, the art of packing – a delicate dance between maximizing space and ensuring your belongings arrive safe and sound. It's a skill that separates the seasoned travelers from the suitcase-bursting novices. But fear not, future packing pro, this subchapter will equip you with the knowledge and strategies to conquer the packing challenge and arrive at your dorm room with everything you need (and nothing you don't).

First, create a master list.

Think of it as your packing bible, a comprehensive inventory of everything you'll need for dorm life. Categorize your list by room (bedroom, bathroom, study area) and prioritize essentials versus "nice-to-haves." Don't forget to include items like bedding, towels, toiletries, study supplies, and those all-important late-night snacking essentials.

Next, embrace the space-saving mindset.

Dorm rooms are notorious for their lack of storage space, so efficiency is key. Utilize packing cubes to organize clothes by category, roll your clothes instead of folding them to save space, and invest in vacuum-sealed bags for bulky items like bedding and towels. Get creative with storage solutions – under-bed storage bins, hanging organizers, and stackable shelves are your new best friends.

Finally, label like a librarian.

Clear and detailed labeling is your secret weapon against unpacking chaos. Label each box with its contents and the room it belongs in. This will not only save you time and frustration on move-in day but also help you avoid the dreaded "mystery box" situation weeks later.

Remember, packing is an art form, a delicate balance between practicality and efficiency. By creating a detailed list, utilizing space-saving techniques, and embracing the power of labeling, you'll transform the packing process from a daunting chore into a satisfying accomplishment. Now go forth and conquer those boxes!

2.3 The Big Day: Conquering Move-In Day

Move-in day – a whirlwind of emotions, logistical Tetris, and the official start of your college journey. It's a day filled with excitement, anticipation, and perhaps a touch of overwhelm as you navigate the campus, haul boxes, and meet your new roommate for the first time. But fear not, future dorm dweller, with a little preparation and a positive attitude, you can conquer move-in day like a seasoned pro.

Think of it as a carefully choreographed dance, each step bringing you closer to creating your home away from home.

First, coordinate with your crew.

Whether you're relying on family, friends, or a team of helpful upperclassmen, ensure everyone is on the same page regarding arrival times, parking logistics, and dorm room assignments. Delegate tasks and communicate clearly to avoid confusion and ensure a smooth process.

Next, embrace the check-in process.

Be prepared to navigate the official check-in procedures, which may involve paperwork, key pick-up, and a brief orientation session. Have your student ID and any necessary documents readily available. Patience is key, as move-in day can be a busy time for everyone involved.

Finally, unpack and personalize.

Once you've hauled your belongings to your new abode, take a deep breath and start unpacking strategically. Refer to your labeled boxes and prioritize essential items first. Unpack bedding, toiletries, and study supplies to create a functional living space. Then, let your personality shine! Decorate your space with photos, posters, and personal touches that make it feel like home.

Remember, move-in day is just the beginning of your college adventure. Embrace the organized chaos, connect with your new roommate and neighbors, and take time to appreciate this exciting milestone. With a positive attitude and a little teamwork, you'll transform your dorm room into a comfortable and inspiring space to call your own.

2.4 Dorm Room Essentials and Hacks: From Functional to Fabulous

Your dorm room is more than just a place to sleep – it's your sanctuary, your study haven, your entertainment hub, and sometimes even your impromptu kitchen. But let's be real, dorm rooms aren't exactly known for their spaciousness or luxurious amenities. Fear not, future interior design extraordinaire, this subchapter is your guide to creating a functional and fabulous dorm room that reflects your personality and maximizes every square inch of space.

Think of it as a creative challenge, an opportunity to transform a blank canvas into a comfortable and inspiring haven that feels like home.

First, equip yourself with the essentials.

Bedding, towels, toiletries – these are the basics that will ensure your comfort and well-being. Invest in a mattress topper for added comfort and consider space-saving solutions like storage ottomans or under-bed storage containers. Don't forget a desk lamp, a comfortable chair, and a reliable power strip to keep all your devices charged and ready for action.

Next, embrace the power of organization.

Dorm rooms can quickly become cluttered, so organization is key. Utilize drawer dividers, hanging organizers, and stackable shelves to maximize storage space. Invest in a shower caddy to keep your bathroom essentials organized and easily transportable to and from the communal bathroom.

Finally, add a touch of personality.

This is your space, so let your personality shine! Decorate with photos, posters, and artwork that inspire you. Add a cozy rug, colorful throw pillows, and fairy lights to create a warm and inviting atmosphere. Don't be afraid to get creative with DIY projects or repurpose old items to add a unique touch to your décor.

Remember, your dorm room is a reflection of you. By combining functional essentials with creative design solutions and personal touches, you'll create a space that not only meets your needs but also inspires and energizes you throughout your college journey.

2.5 Safety and Security: Protecting Your Personal Haven

Amidst the excitement of decorating your dorm room and embracing college life, it's crucial to prioritize your safety and the security of your belongings. While college campuses are generally safe environments, it's always wise to be proactive and take necessary precautions to protect yourself and your possessions.

Think of it as building a fortress of awareness and preparedness, ensuring your peace of mind and creating a secure environment where you can thrive.

First, familiarize yourself with campus safety protocols.

Understand emergency procedures, evacuation routes, and the location of campus security offices. Download the campus safety app, if available, for quick access to emergency contacts and safety alerts. Attend any safety orientations or workshops offered by the university to gain valuable knowledge and resources.

Next, secure your dorm room.

Always lock your door, even if you're just stepping out for a moment. Consider investing in a personal safe or lockbox to store valuables like passports, jewelry, or important documents. Be mindful of who you allow into your dorm room and avoid propping doors open for extended periods.

Finally, be aware of your surroundings.

Trust your instincts and avoid walking alone at night, especially in poorly lit areas. Utilize campus escort services or buddy systems when necessary. Be cautious about sharing personal information online or with strangers, and report any suspicious activity to campus security immediately.

Remember, safety is a shared responsibility. By staying informed, taking precautions, and looking out for yourself and others, you contribute to a secure and welcoming campus environment for everyone.

Chapter 3: Building Your Nest: Creating a Home Away from Home

"Home is not a place...it's a feeling." - Cecilia Ahern

The boxes are unpacked, the décor is in place, and your dorm room is starting to feel like your own. But creating a true home away from home goes beyond furniture and fairy lights – it's about fostering a sense of belonging, building meaningful connections, and establishing routines that support your well-being. This chapter delves into the heart of creating a nurturing and comfortable environment where you can thrive both personally and academically.

We'll explore the art of roommate relationships, delve into organization and time management strategies, and guide you on building a sense of community within the larger campus ecosystem. Get ready to transform your dorm room from a mere living space into a true home, a foundation for growth, connection, and unforgettable college experiences.

3.1 Personalizing Your Space: From Blank Canvas to Cozy Haven

Your dorm room is more than just four walls and a bed – it's your personal sanctuary within the bustling world of college life. It's where you'll unwind after a long day of classes, recharge for upcoming exams, and create lasting memories with friends. Transforming this blank canvas into a cozy and inspiring haven is an essential step in feeling truly at home on campus.

Think of it as an opportunity to express your unique personality and create a space that reflects your style, interests, and aspirations.

First, infuse your space with personal touches.

Photos of loved ones, cherished mementos, and artwork that speaks to you – these are the elements that will transform your dorm room from generic to uniquely yours. Consider creating a vision board showcasing your goals and dreams, or a photo wall that celebrates your favorite memories and the people who matter most.

Next, prioritize comfort and functionality.

Invest in a cozy rug, soft blankets, and plush pillows to create a welcoming and relaxing atmosphere. Ensure your study area is well-lit and organized, with a comfortable chair and ample desk space. Add storage solutions like shelves, bins, and organizers to keep your belongings tidy and maximize space.

Finally, embrace the power of lighting.

Harsh fluorescent lights can zap the energy out of any space. Opt for warm, ambient lighting with fairy lights, string lights, or a Himalayan salt lamp. A bedside lamp with a dimmer switch allows you to adjust the lighting for reading or creating a relaxing atmosphere before sleep.

Remember, your dorm room is a reflection of you. By infusing it with personal touches, prioritizing comfort, and creating a warm and inviting ambiance, you'll transform your space into a sanctuary that nurtures your well-being and inspires you throughout your college journey.

3.2 Roommate Harmony: Building a Respectful and Supportive Cohabitation

Living with a roommate can be one of the most rewarding and challenging aspects of the college experience. It's an opportunity to forge a close bond, share late-night laughs, and navigate the ups and downs of college life together. However, it also requires compromise, communication, and a healthy dose of respect for each other's needs and boundaries.

Think of it as a crash course in interpersonal relationships, a chance to develop valuable communication and conflict-resolution skills that will serve you well beyond your dorm room walls.

First, establish open and honest communication.

From the outset, discuss expectations, preferences, and potential concerns. Do you prefer a quiet study environment or enjoy background music? Are you an early riser or a night owl? Open communication is key to avoiding misunderstandings and ensuring a harmonious living situation.

Next, set boundaries and ground rules.

Discuss shared responsibilities like cleaning, guest policies, and noise levels. Establish boundaries regarding personal belongings, study time, and alone time. Be respectful of each other's schedules and preferences, and communicate any concerns openly and honestly.

Finally, embrace compromise and conflict resolution.

Disagreements are inevitable in any shared living situation. The key is to address them respectfully and find solutions that work for both parties. Practice active listening, express your needs clearly, and be willing to compromise.

Remember, building a positive roommate relationship takes time and effort. By prioritizing communication, respecting boundaries, and embracing compromise, you can create a supportive and harmonious living environment that enhances your overall college experience.

3.3 Conquering Chaos: Organization and Time Management Strategies

College life is a whirlwind of classes, social events, extracurricular activities, and the occasional late-night pizza run. Amidst this exciting chaos, staying organized and managing your time effectively is crucial for maintaining your sanity and achieving academic success.

Think of it as a juggling act, where you're the skilled performer keeping multiple balls in the air with grace and precision.

First, establish a system for organization.

Invest in a planner, whether it's a physical notebook or a digital app, and use it religiously. Schedule your classes, study sessions, extracurricular activities, and social events. Create to-do lists and prioritize tasks based on deadlines and importance.

Next, tame the paper tiger.

Develop a system for organizing your notes, handouts, and assignments. Consider color-coding by subject, using binders with dividers, or creating digital folders on your laptop. Establish a designated study space that is free from distractions and conducive to focus.

Finally, master the art of time management.

Break down large assignments into smaller, manageable tasks. Utilize time-blocking techniques to allocate specific time slots for studying, socializing, and personal errands. Avoid procrastination by setting realistic deadlines and rewarding yourself for completing tasks.

Remember, effective organization and time management are not about rigid schedules or strict routines – they're about creating systems that work for you and allow you to navigate the demands of college life with ease and efficiency.

3.4 Finding Your Tribe: Building a Community on Campus

College is more than just academics – it's an opportunity to explore your interests, discover new passions, and connect with like-minded individuals who will become your lifelong friends and support system. Building a sense of community on campus is essential for feeling truly at home and maximizing your college experience.

Think of it as a grand adventure, where you'll embark on a quest to find your tribe, those individuals who share your values, interests, and that unique brand of college humor.

First, explore campus activities and organizations.

From academic clubs to sports teams to volunteer groups, there's something for everyone on a college campus. Attend club fairs, browse online directories, and talk to upperclassmen to discover organizations that align with your interests. Stepping outside your comfort zone and trying new things is a fantastic way to meet new people and discover hidden passions.

Next, connect with classmates through shared interests.

Strike up conversations with classmates in your dorm, at the library, or during social events. Bond over shared academic struggles, favorite TV shows, or a mutual love for late-night pizza runs. These casual connections can blossom into meaningful friendships that enrich your college experience.

Finally, explore the surrounding community.

Venture beyond the campus bubble and discover the hidden gems of your college town or city. Visit local coffee shops, explore museums and art galleries, or volunteer at a community organization. Engaging with the local community is a fantastic way to broaden your horizons and meet people from diverse backgrounds.

Remember, building a community takes time and effort. By actively participating in campus life, connecting with classmates, and exploring your surroundings, you'll create a network of support, friendship, and belonging that will make your college experience truly unforgettable.

3.5 From Dependent to Independent: Fostering Responsibility and Self-Reliance

College is a transformative period, a bridge between the dependence of adolescence and the independence of adulthood. It's a time to develop essential life skills, take ownership of your decisions, and cultivate a sense of self-reliance that will serve you well beyond your college years.

Think of it as a personal growth spurt, where you'll shed the training wheels and learn to navigate the world with confidence and autonomy.

First, master the art of adulting.

Laundry, cooking, cleaning – these may not be the most glamorous tasks, but they're essential life skills that every independent adult should possess. Embrace the opportunity to learn how to do your own laundry (without turning everything pink), whip up a simple meal (beyond instant ramen), and maintain a clean and organized living space.

Next, take ownership of your academics.

College is a self-directed learning environment, where success depends on your ability to manage your time, prioritize tasks, and seek help when needed. Develop effective study habits, attend classes regularly, and communicate with professors if you're struggling. Remember, your academic success is ultimately in your hands.

Finally, cultivate a sense of financial responsibility.

Create a budget, track your expenses, and avoid unnecessary debt. Explore opportunities for part-time work or freelance gigs to supplement your income and gain valuable work experience. Learn to make informed financial decisions that support your current needs and future goals.

Remember, independence is not about doing everything on your own – it's about taking responsibility for your actions, learning from your mistakes, and developing the confidence to navigate life's challenges with resilience and resourcefulness.

Chapter 4: Academic Success: Strategies for Thriving in College

"Education is the most powerful weapon which you can use to change the world." - Nelson Mandela

The thrill of college life extends far beyond dorm room decorations and late-night pizza runs. At its core lies the pursuit of knowledge, the expansion of your intellectual horizons, and the development of skills that will shape your future. This chapter delves into the heart of academic success, equipping you with strategies to navigate the academic landscape, master the art of studying, and thrive in the intellectually stimulating environment of college.

We'll explore effective study techniques, delve into the importance of building relationships with professors, and guide you on achieving a healthy balance between academic pursuits and the social aspects of college life. Get ready to unlock your full academic potential and embark on a journey of intellectual discovery and personal growth.

4.1 Navigating the Academic Landscape: Understanding the System

Stepping into the world of college academics can feel like entering a new country with its own unique language, customs, and expectations. From deciphering course registration systems to understanding credit hours and grading policies, it's essential to familiarize yourself with the academic landscape of your college to ensure a smooth and successful transition.

Think of it as decoding a secret map, unlocking the knowledge and strategies needed to navigate the academic terrain with confidence.

First, decipher the course registration system.

Each college has its own unique system for course registration, often involving online portals, specific enrollment periods, and a hierarchy of registration priorities. Familiarize yourself with the process well in advance to ensure you secure your desired courses and avoid any last-minute scrambling.

Next, understand credit hours and graduation requirements.

Credit hours determine the workload and academic weight of each course. Ensure you understand how many credits are required for graduation and how they are distributed across different disciplines and elective options. Consult with your academic advisor to create a course plan that aligns with your academic goals and graduation timeline.

Finally, explore academic resources and support services.

Colleges offer a wealth of resources to support student success, including libraries, tutoring centers, writing labs, and academic advising offices. Take advantage of these services early on to develop effective study habits, improve your writing skills, and seek guidance on academic challenges.

Remember, navigating the academic landscape is an ongoing process. By understanding the system, utilizing available resources, and seeking support when needed, you'll set yourself up for academic success and a fulfilling college experience.

4.2 Cracking the Study Code: Mastering the Art of Learning

Gone are the days of passively absorbing information and regurgitating facts on exams. College-level learning requires a more active and engaged approach, one that involves critical thinking, analysis, and the ability to apply knowledge to real-world situations. Mastering the art of studying is essential for academic success and intellectual growth.

Think of it as unlocking a treasure chest of learning strategies, each one offering a unique key to unlocking your full academic potential.

First, explore different study techniques.

Experiment with various methods, such as active recall, spaced repetition, and interleaving, to discover what works best for you. Active recall involves retrieving information from memory without looking at your notes, while spaced repetition involves reviewing material at increasing intervals to improve long-term retention. Interleaving involves mixing up different subjects or topics during a study session to enhance understanding and prevent boredom.

Next, embrace the power of active learning.

Instead of passively reading textbooks, engage with the material by taking notes, creating summaries, or participating in study groups. Discussing concepts with peers can deepen your understanding and expose you to different perspectives.

Finally, utilize technology and online resources.

Explore educational apps, online courses, and study guides to supplement your learning. Many universities offer access to online databases and academic journals, providing a wealth of information beyond traditional textbooks.

Remember, effective studying is not about cramming information or spending countless hours hunched over textbooks – it's about finding strategies that work for you and that promote deep understanding, critical thinking, and long-term retention. By embracing active learning and experimenting with different techniques, you'll unlock your full potential as a learner and achieve academic success.

4.3 Professors as Allies: Building Relationships for Success

Professors are more than just lecturers – they are mentors, guides, and potential advocates for your academic and professional journey. Building strong relationships with your professors can open doors to research opportunities, internships, and invaluable guidance in your chosen field.

Think of them as allies in your academic quest, individuals invested in your intellectual growth and eager to share their knowledge and expertise.

First, make your presence known.

Actively participate in class discussions, ask thoughtful questions, and demonstrate your genuine interest in the subject matter. Introduce yourself to your professors during office hours and express your enthusiasm for the course. These small gestures can make a lasting impression and set the foundation for a meaningful connection.

Next, seek guidance and mentorship.

Professors are experts in their fields and can offer invaluable insights and advice. Seek their guidance on academic challenges, career paths, and research opportunities. Their mentorship can provide direction and clarity as you navigate the academic landscape and explore potential career options.

Finally, stay connected beyond the classroom.

Attend departmental events, guest lectures, and conferences where you can interact with professors in a more informal setting. Connect with them on professional networking platforms like LinkedIn to stay updated on their research and potential opportunities.

Remember, building relationships with professors takes time and effort. By demonstrating your engagement, seeking their guidance, and staying connected, you'll cultivate valuable connections that can enhance your academic experience and open doors to future opportunities.

4.4 Balancing Act: Juggling Academics and Social Life

College life is a vibrant tapestry woven from academic pursuits, social engagements, extracurricular activities, and perhaps a few too many late-night study sessions. Achieving a healthy balance between academics and social life is essential for maintaining your well-being, preventing burnout, and maximizing your overall college experience.

Think of it as a seesaw, where you strive to find equilibrium between the demands of academic rigor and the enriching experiences of social connection and personal exploration.

First, prioritize academics without sacrificing your social life.

Create a schedule that allocates dedicated time for both studying and socializing. Avoid procrastination by setting realistic deadlines and breaking down large tasks into smaller, manageable chunks. This will free up time for social engagements without compromising your academic performance.

Next, say "no" without feeling guilty.

It's impossible to attend every party, club meeting, or social gathering. Learn to prioritize events that align with your interests and values, and politely decline invitations when you need time for studying, self-care, or simply recharging your batteries.

Finally, embrace the power of "me time."

Amidst the hustle and bustle of college life, it's essential to carve out time for yourself. Engage in activities that bring you joy and help you de-stress, whether it's reading a good book, going for a run, or simply enjoying a quiet cup of coffee.

Remember, balance is not about dividing your time equally between academics and social life – it's about finding a rhythm that works for you and allows you to thrive in both areas. By prioritizing your well-being, setting boundaries, and embracing the power of "no," you'll create a fulfilling and balanced college experience.

4.5 Overcoming Academic Hurdles: Bouncing Back from Setbacks

The path to academic success is rarely a smooth one. There will be challenging courses, unexpected setbacks, and moments of self-doubt. The key is to develop resilience, seek support when needed, and view these challenges as opportunities for growth and learning.

Think of it as navigating a winding road, where occasional bumps and detours ultimately lead you to your destination.

First, recognize the signs of academic struggle.

Falling behind in coursework, declining grades, or feeling overwhelmed by academic demands are all indicators that you may need additional support. Don't wait until you're drowning in assignments or facing academic probation – seek help early on.

Next, utilize available resources.

Colleges offer a wealth of academic support services, including tutoring centers, writing labs, and academic advising. Take advantage of these resources to improve your study skills, receive guidance on challenging coursework, and develop strategies for academic success.

Finally, cultivate a growth mindset.

View setbacks as opportunities for learning and improvement. Instead of dwelling on failures, focus on identifying areas for growth and developing strategies to overcome challenges. Embrace a positive attitude and believe in your ability to succeed.

Remember, academic challenges are a normal part of the college experience. By recognizing the signs of struggle, seeking support, and developing a growth mindset, you'll build resilience, overcome obstacles, and emerge stronger and more capable than ever before.

Chapter 5: Wellness and Self-Care: Prioritizing Your Well-being

"Self-care is not selfish. You cannot serve from an empty vessel." - Eleanor Brown

College life is an exhilarating whirlwind of academic pursuits, social engagements, and new experiences. However, amidst the excitement and challenges, it's crucial to prioritize your well-being and make time for self-care. This chapter delves into the importance of nurturing your physical, mental, and emotional health to ensure you thrive throughout your college journey.

Think of it as building a strong foundation for success, ensuring you have the energy, resilience, and mental clarity to navigate the demands of college life and emerge as your best self.

We'll explore strategies for maintaining physical health, managing stress and anxiety, building healthy relationships, and cultivating a positive mindset. Get ready to embark on a journey of self-discovery and prioritize your well-being as an essential ingredient for a fulfilling and successful college experience.

5.1 Fueling Your Body and Mind: Maintaining Physical Health

College life can be a recipe for unhealthy habits – late-night study sessions fueled by junk food, skipped meals in the rush between classes, and a general disregard for exercise amidst the chaos of deadlines and social engagements. However, prioritizing your physical health is crucial for maintaining energy levels, boosting cognitive function, and supporting your overall well-being.

Think of your body as a high-performance machine – it needs the right fuel and regular maintenance to function at its best.

First, navigate the dining hall jungle.

College dining halls offer a smorgasbord of options, from healthy salads and lean proteins to greasy pizza and mountains of dessert. Make informed choices by focusing on fruits, vegetables, whole grains, and lean protein sources. Limit processed foods, sugary drinks, and excessive amounts of unhealthy fats.

Next, incorporate exercise into your routine.

You don't need a fancy gym membership or a personal trainer to stay active. Take advantage of campus fitness facilities, join a recreational sports team, or simply go for a run or bike ride around campus. Even small amounts of physical activity can boost your mood, improve sleep quality, and enhance cognitive function.

Finally, prioritize sleep.

College schedules can be erratic, but strive to establish a consistent sleep routine. Aim for 7-8 hours of quality sleep each night to ensure you're well-rested and able to focus during the day. Avoid late-night screen time, create a relaxing bedtime ritual, and establish a regular sleep-wake cycle.

Remember, physical health is the foundation for overall well-being. By nourishing your body with healthy foods, engaging in regular exercise, and prioritizing sleep, you'll create a strong and resilient foundation for academic success and a fulfilling college experience.

5.2 Taming the Mental Monsters: Managing Stress and Anxiety

College life is an emotional rollercoaster, filled with exhilarating highs and challenging lows. The pressure to succeed academically, navigate new social situations, and manage newfound independence can take a toll on your mental health. Learning to manage stress and anxiety is crucial for maintaining emotional well-being and preventing burnout.

Think of it as taming the mental monsters that can lurk in the shadows, equipping yourself with tools and strategies to navigate challenging emotions and maintain a sense of calm amidst the chaos.

First, recognize the signs of stress and anxiety.

Difficulty concentrating, changes in sleep patterns, irritability, and feelings of overwhelm are all indicators that your mental health may be suffering. Don't ignore these signs – acknowledge them and take steps to address them before they escalate.

Next, develop coping mechanisms.

Explore stress-reduction techniques such as deep breathing exercises, meditation, yoga, or journaling. Engaging in physical activity, spending time in nature, and connecting with supportive friends and family can also help alleviate stress and anxiety.

Finally, seek professional help if needed.

College campuses offer mental health services through counseling centers and student support groups. Don't hesitate to reach out for professional help if you're struggling to manage stress, anxiety, or other mental health concerns. There's no shame in seeking support – in fact, it's a sign of strength and self-awareness.

Remember, mental health is just as important as physical health. By acknowledging your emotions, developing coping mechanisms, and seeking support when needed, you'll build resilience, manage stress effectively, and cultivate a sense of inner peace amidst the challenges of college life.

5.3 Building Healthy Relationships: Fostering Connection and Support

College is a time for forging new friendships, exploring romantic relationships, and building a network of support that will extend far beyond your campus years. However, navigating the complexities of social dynamics and establishing healthy relationships requires effort, communication, and a commitment to mutual respect and understanding.

Think of it as cultivating a garden of connection, nurturing positive relationships that provide support, encouragement, and a sense of belonging.

First, surround yourself with positive influences.

Seek out friends who uplift and inspire you, who share your values and support your goals. Distance yourself from toxic relationships or individuals who drain your energy and bring negativity into your life.

Next, prioritize open and honest communication.

Express your needs and expectations clearly, and listen actively to the perspectives of others. Be willing to compromise and find solutions that work for both parties. Healthy relationships are built on a foundation of mutual respect, understanding, and open communication.

Finally, set boundaries and respect the boundaries of others.

It's okay to say "no" to requests or invitations that don't align with your values or priorities. Respect the boundaries set by others, and communicate your own boundaries clearly and assertively.

Remember, healthy relationships are essential for your well-being and contribute to a positive college experience. By surrounding yourself with positive influences, prioritizing communication, and respecting boundaries, you'll cultivate meaningful connections that enrich your life and provide support throughout your college journey and beyond.

5.4 Home Is Where the Heart Is: Staying Connected with Loved Ones

Leaving home for college can be a bittersweet experience, filled with excitement for new adventures and a tinge of sadness as you say goodbye to family and friends. Maintaining connections with loved ones back home is crucial for emotional well-being and a sense of grounding amidst the whirlwind of college life.

Think of it as building bridges across the distance, nurturing the bonds that provide comfort, support, and a sense of belonging even when miles apart.

First, prioritize regular communication.

Schedule phone calls, video chats, or even old-fashioned handwritten letters to stay in touch with family and friends. Share your experiences, challenges, and triumphs with them, and actively listen to their updates and stories. Regular communication will help maintain a sense of closeness and connection, even across the miles.

Next, plan visits home.

Whether it's for holidays, semester breaks, or simply a weekend getaway, make time to visit home and reconnect with loved ones in person. These visits provide an opportunity to recharge, reminisce, and strengthen the bonds that may have felt strained by distance.

Finally, embrace technology.

Social media platforms, messaging apps, and video conferencing tools provide convenient ways to stay connected with loved ones on a daily basis. Share photos and videos, send funny memes, or simply check in with a quick message to let them know you're thinking of them.

Remember, even though you're embarking on a new chapter in your life, the connections you have with family and friends back home remain an essential part of your support system. By prioritizing communication, planning visits, and embracing technology, you'll maintain strong bonds and ensure that home is always just a phone call, video chat, or plane ride away.

5.5 Cultivating Optimism: The Power of a Positive Mindset

College life is full of ups and downs, moments of triumph and inevitable setbacks. Maintaining a positive mindset is crucial for navigating challenges, overcoming obstacles, and thriving in the face of adversity.

Think of it as a mental shield, deflecting negativity and empowering you to approach life with optimism and resilience.

First, practice gratitude.

Take time each day to reflect on the things you're grateful for, whether it's supportive friends, a challenging but rewarding class, or simply a sunny day. Focusing on the positive aspects of your life can shift your perspective and foster a sense of appreciation for the good things, big and small.

Next, challenge negative thoughts.

When self-doubt or negativity creeps in, challenge those thoughts with evidence to the contrary. Focus on your strengths, past successes, and the progress you've made. Replace negative self-talk with positive affirmations and empowering beliefs.

Finally, embrace a growth mindset.

View challenges as opportunities for learning and growth. Instead of fearing failure, embrace it as a stepping stone on the path to success. Believe in your ability to learn, adapt, and overcome obstacles.

Remember, a positive mindset is not about ignoring challenges or pretending everything is perfect – it's about choosing to focus on the good, learning from setbacks, and approaching life with optimism and resilience. By cultivating a positive mindset, you'll empower yourself to thrive in college and beyond.

Chapter 6: Navigating Social Life and Campus Culture

"We are like islands in the sea, separate on the surface but connected in the deep." - William James

College is more than just academics; it's a vibrant tapestry of social experiences, cultural immersion, and the forging of lifelong connections. This chapter delves into the exciting realm of social life and campus culture, guiding you through the process of making friends, navigating social events, and embracing the unique traditions and opportunities that your college has to offer.

Think of it as a grand social experiment, a chance to step outside your comfort zone, discover new interests, and connect with individuals from diverse backgrounds and perspectives.

We'll explore strategies for building friendships, navigating the college dating scene, partying responsibly, and embracing diversity and inclusion within the campus community. Get ready to dive into the social whirl of college life and create unforgettable memories that will last a lifetime.

6.1 Decoding the Social Scene: Exploring Campus Culture

Stepping onto a college campus is like entering a new world with its own unique language, traditions, and social norms. From football rivalries and quirky mascots to annual festivals and late-night study rituals, each college cultivates a distinct culture that shapes the student experience. Understanding and embracing this culture is essential for feeling like you belong and making the most of your time on campus.

Think of it as cracking a cultural code, deciphering the unspoken rules and traditions that define your college community.

First, immerse yourself in campus traditions.

Attend sporting events, participate in homecoming festivities, and explore the history and legends that make your college unique. These traditions foster a sense of community and shared identity, connecting you to generations of students who have walked the same paths and cheered for the same teams.

Next, discover the social landscape.

Explore the various social groups, clubs, and organizations on campus. Attend club fairs, browse online directories, and talk to upperclassmen to gain insights into the social dynamics and find groups that align with your interests.

Finally, observe and adapt.

Pay attention to the unspoken social norms and etiquette on campus. Observe how students interact with each other, professors, and staff. Adapt your behavior to fit the culture while still staying true to your own values and personality.

Remember, campus culture is dynamic and ever-evolving. By immersing yourself in traditions, exploring the social landscape, and observing social norms, you'll gain a deeper understanding of your college community and find your place within it.

6.2 From Classmates to Companions: Making Friends and Building Connections

College is a melting pot of individuals from diverse backgrounds, interests, and perspectives. It's a prime opportunity to expand your social circle, forge lasting friendships, and build a network of support that will enrich your college experience and beyond.

Think of it as a treasure hunt, where every interaction holds the potential for discovering a hidden gem of friendship and connection.

First, step outside your comfort zone.

Strike up conversations with classmates, dorm neighbors, or individuals you meet at campus events. Introduce yourself, ask questions, and show genuine interest in getting to know others. Remember, everyone is in the same boat, navigating a new environment and seeking connection.

Next, explore shared interests.

Join clubs and organizations that align with your passions, whether it's a sports team, a debate club, or a volunteer group. Participating in activities you enjoy is a fantastic way to meet like-minded individuals and build friendships based on shared interests.

Finally, be open to unexpected connections.

Some of the most meaningful friendships blossom from unexpected encounters. Don't limit yourself to a specific social group or stereotype. Embrace diversity and be open to connecting with individuals from different backgrounds and walks of life.

Remember, building friendships takes time and effort. By stepping outside your comfort zone, exploring shared interests, and embracing openness, you'll cultivate a network of friends who will support you, challenge you, and create lasting memories throughout your college journey.

6.3 Navigating the Dating Game: Relationships in the College Realm

College often becomes a playground for exploration, not just academically, but also romantically. The influx of new faces and experiences creates a unique landscape for navigating the complexities of dating and relationships. This period of self-discovery offers a prime opportunity to understand your own values, explore different relationship dynamics, and build connections that range from casual to committed.

Think of it as a crash course in relationship building, where you'll learn valuable lessons about communication, boundaries, and emotional intelligence.

Understanding the Evolving Landscape: The college dating scene is a diverse ecosystem, encompassing everything from casual hookups to serious relationships. It's essential to be upfront about your own intentions and expectations while also respecting the choices of others. Remember, there's no one-size-fits-all approach to dating – it's about discovering what works for you and prioritizing your own emotional well-being.

Communication is Key: Regardless of whether you're casually dating or in a committed relationship, open and honest communication is the cornerstone of any healthy connection.

Express your needs, boundaries, and expectations clearly, and actively listen to your partner's perspective. Honest communication fosters trust, understanding, and a sense of mutual respect.

Maintaining a Healthy Balance: Amidst the excitement of new relationships and the whirlwind of college life, it's crucial to maintain a healthy balance between your romantic life, academics, friendships, and personal growth. Avoid neglecting other aspects of your life in favor of a new relationship, and ensure you're dedicating sufficient time and energy to your studies, personal goals, and existing social connections.

Respect and Consent are Non-Negotiable: College dating should always be rooted in respect and consent. Ensure you have clear and enthusiastic consent from your partner before engaging in any physical intimacy. Understand and respect personal boundaries, and be mindful of the impact your words and actions can have on others. Remember, healthy relationships are built on a foundation of mutual respect, trust, and understanding.

Navigating Challenges and Conflict: Disagreements and challenges are inevitable in any relationship. The key is to approach conflict with maturity and a willingness to find solutions that work for both parties. Practice active listening, express your concerns openly and honestly, and be willing to compromise. Seek support from friends, family, or campus resources if needed, and remember that healthy relationships require effort, understanding, and a commitment to growth.

Dating and Mental Health: It's important to acknowledge the impact that dating and relationships can have on your mental health. If you experience anxiety, insecurity, or emotional distress related to your dating life, seek support from friends, family, or mental health professionals. Remember, prioritizing your emotional well-being is crucial for building healthy and fulfilling relationships.

Embrace the Journey: College dating is a unique and often transformative experience. Approach it with an open mind, a willingness to learn, and a focus on personal growth. Celebrate the joys of connection, learn from challenges, and embrace the journey of discovering what you truly value in a partner and a relationship.

6.4 Partying Smart: Balancing Fun with Responsibility

College is often synonymous with a vibrant social scene, where parties and social gatherings become a cornerstone of the student experience. While these events offer opportunities for fun, connection, and stress relief, it's crucial to approach them with a sense of responsibility and awareness of potential risks.

Think of it as a balancing act, where you can enjoy the social aspects of college life while also prioritizing your safety, well-being, and academic success.

Understanding the Risks: Alcohol and drug use are prevalent on many college campuses, but it's essential to understand the potential risks associated with substance abuse. Excessive alcohol consumption can lead to impaired judgment, risky behavior, and even alcohol poisoning. Drug use carries its own set of risks, including addiction, legal consequences, and negative impacts on physical and mental health.

Setting Boundaries and Knowing Your Limits: Before attending social events, establish clear boundaries for yourself regarding alcohol or drug use. Know your limits and stick to them. Avoid feeling pressured to engage in substance use if you're uncomfortable, and have a plan for getting home safely if you choose to consume alcohol.

Partying with a Buddy System: Never attend parties or social events alone, especially if alcohol or drugs are involved. Have a trusted friend or group of friends who will look out for you and ensure you get home safely. Establish a check-in system or designate a sober friend who can provide support and assistance if needed.

Staying Hydrated and Nourished: If you choose to consume alcohol, be sure to stay hydrated by drinking plenty of water throughout the night. Eating a meal before or during the event can also help slow down alcohol absorption and reduce the risk of intoxication.

Respecting Others and Yourself: Parties and social events should be a source of fun and enjoyment for everyone involved. Treat others with respect, avoid engaging in risky or harmful behavior, and prioritize your own safety and well-being. Remember, it's okay to say "no" if you're uncomfortable with any situation or activity.

Seeking Help When Needed: If you or someone you know is struggling with substance abuse, seek help from campus resources, such as counseling centers, student health services, or support groups. There is no shame in asking for help, and early intervention can make a significant difference in preventing long-term consequences.

Remember, partying smart is about making informed choices, prioritizing your well-being, and respecting yourself and others. By balancing fun with responsibility, you can enjoy the social aspects of college life while also ensuring your safety and academic success.

6.5 Embracing Diversity and Inclusion: Building a Welcoming Community

College campuses are melting pots of diverse backgrounds, perspectives, and experiences. Embracing this diversity and fostering an inclusive environment where everyone feels valued and respected is essential for creating a thriving and enriching college community.

Think of it as a vibrant tapestry, woven from unique threads of culture, identity, and lived experiences, each contributing to the richness and beauty of the whole.

Respecting Differences: Acknowledge and celebrate the diversity of your peers. Learn about different cultures, religions, and perspectives, and approach interactions with an open mind and a willingness to understand. Avoid making assumptions or generalizations based on stereotypes, and treat everyone with respect and dignity.

Challenging Bias and Discrimination: Be aware of your own biases and actively work to challenge them. Speak out against discrimination or prejudice, whether it's based on race, ethnicity, gender, sexual orientation, religion, or any other personal characteristic. Contribute to creating a campus environment where everyone feels safe, valued, and empowered to be their authentic selves.

Promoting Inclusive Language: Use inclusive language that avoids stereotypes or generalizations. Be mindful of the pronouns people use to identify themselves, and respect their preferred terms. Language has the power to create a welcoming and inclusive environment or to perpetuate exclusion and discrimination.

Engaging in Dialogue: Participate in conversations about diversity and inclusion. Attend campus events, workshops, or lectures that explore issues related to social justice, equity, and cultural understanding. Engage in open and respectful dialogue with peers from diverse backgrounds to broaden your perspective and challenge your own assumptions.

Supporting Inclusive Initiatives: Get involved in campus organizations or initiatives that promote diversity and inclusion. Volunteer your time, attend events, or simply show your support for efforts that create a more welcoming and equitable campus community.

Remember, creating an inclusive environment is an ongoing process that requires effort, awareness, and a commitment to challenging bias and promoting understanding. By respecting differences, challenging discrimination, and actively promoting inclusion, you contribute to a campus culture where everyone feels valued and empowered to thrive.

Chapter 7: Beyond the Campus: Exploring Your Surroundings

"Not all those who wander are lost." - J.R.R. Tolkien

While college life often revolves around the campus bubble, a world of exploration and adventure awaits just beyond those familiar walls. This chapter encourages you to venture beyond the confines of your academic environment and discover the hidden gems of your college town or city, immersing yourself in the local culture and expanding your horizons beyond the classroom.

Think of it as an expedition into uncharted territory, a chance to broaden your perspective, discover new interests, and create lasting memories.

We'll delve into the art of navigating your surroundings, from utilizing public transportation to planning weekend adventures and exploring career opportunities in the local community. Get ready to embark on a journey of discovery and experience all that your college town or city has to offer.

7.1 Discovering Hidden Gems: Exploring the Local Community

Beyond the familiar pathways of campus lies a world waiting to be explored – your college town or city, brimming with its own unique culture, history, and hidden gems. Venturing off-campus is not just about escaping the academic bubble; it's an opportunity to broaden your horizons, connect with the local community, and discover new interests and experiences.

Think of it as an urban (or rural) exploration, a chance to unearth the treasures that lie beyond the campus gates.

First, delve into the local culture.

Visit museums, art galleries, and historical landmarks to immerse yourself in the history and heritage of your college town. Explore local shops, restaurants, and cafes to experience the unique flavors and ambiance of the community. Attend local festivals, farmers markets, and cultural events to gain a deeper understanding of the local customs and traditions.

Next, seek out hidden gems.

Venture beyond the tourist hotspots and discover the lesser-known treasures of your surroundings. Explore local parks, hiking trails, or scenic waterways. Discover independent bookstores, record shops, or vintage clothing stores that offer a unique and eclectic shopping experience. Seek out hidden cafes, cozy pubs, or live music venues that cater to the local crowd.

Finally, connect with the community.

Volunteer your time at a local organization, attend community events, or simply strike up conversations with locals at coffee shops or parks. Engaging with the community is a rewarding way to give back, broaden your perspective, and build meaningful connections beyond the campus bubble.

Remember, your college town or city is an extension of your campus experience. By exploring the local culture, seeking out hidden gems, and connecting with the community, you'll create lasting memories and enrich your college journey in countless ways.

7.2 Navigating the Urban Jungle: Transportation and Getting Around

Venturing beyond the campus bubble often requires navigating the transportation landscape of your college town or city. Whether it's hopping on a bus, catching a train, or zipping around on a bike, understanding your transportation options is essential for exploring your surroundings with ease and efficiency.

Think of it as unlocking the secrets of urban (or rural) mobility, ensuring you can reach your destination without getting lost in the transportation maze.

First, explore public transportation options.

Most college towns and cities offer a network of buses, trains, or subways. Familiarize yourself with the routes, schedules, and fare systems. Many universities offer discounted transit passes for students, providing an affordable and convenient way to get around.

Next, consider alternative transportation modes.

Biking is a popular and eco-friendly way to navigate college towns, offering exercise and the freedom to explore at your own pace. Many cities have bike-sharing programs or designated bike lanes for safe and convenient cycling. Walking is another option for shorter distances, allowing you to soak up the sights and sounds of your surroundings.

Finally, utilize ride-sharing services.

Companies like Uber and Lyft offer convenient transportation options, especially for late-night outings or trips to areas not well-served by public transit. Be mindful of surge pricing during peak hours, and consider carpooling with friends to share costs.

Remember, getting around your college town or city doesn't have to be a daunting task. By exploring public transportation options, embracing alternative modes of transport, and utilizing ride-sharing services, you'll navigate the urban jungle with ease and unlock a world of exploration beyond the campus gates.

7.3 Weekend Wanderlust: Planning Adventures and Exploring Beyond

College life is more than just attending classes and studying – it's also an opportunity to explore new places, embark on spontaneous adventures, and create lasting memories with friends. Weekend getaways and excursions beyond your college town offer a chance to escape the academic bubble, broaden your horizons, and experience different cultures and landscapes.

Think of it as a mini-vacation, a chance to recharge your batteries and return to campus feeling refreshed and inspired.

First, gather your travel crew.

Coordinate with friends who share your sense of adventure and wanderlust. Discuss interests, budget constraints, and preferred travel styles to ensure a compatible and enjoyable experience for everyone.

Next, choose your destination.

Research nearby cities, national parks, or scenic areas within driving distance or a short flight. Consider your interests – whether it's exploring historical landmarks, hiking in nature, or soaking up the sun on a beach – and choose a destination that caters to your preferences.

Finally, plan your itinerary.

Research attractions, accommodations, and transportation options in advance. Book your flights or rental car, secure lodging, and create a rough itinerary that balances sightseeing with downtime and spontaneous exploration.

Remember, weekend adventures are a chance to break free from routine, create lasting memories, and discover the world beyond your college campus. By planning thoughtfully, embracing spontaneity, and sharing the experience with friends, you'll return to college feeling refreshed, inspired, and ready to tackle the next academic challenge.

7.4 Financial Independence: Budgeting Beyond the Campus Bubble

Venturing beyond the campus often involves additional expenses, from transportation and meals to entertainment and weekend getaways. Maintaining financial responsibility while exploring your surroundings is crucial for avoiding unnecessary debt and ensuring a balanced college experience.

Think of it as a financial balancing act, where you can enjoy the freedom of off-campus excursions while also staying within your budget and making informed spending choices.

First, factor off-campus expenses into your budget.

Allocate a specific amount of money for transportation, meals, entertainment, and other off-campus activities. Track your spending carefully to ensure you're staying within your budget and avoid overspending.

Next, explore opportunities to supplement your income.

Consider part-time jobs, freelance gigs, or on-campus work-study programs to earn extra cash and gain valuable work experience. Be mindful of balancing work commitments with your academic schedule and personal well-being.

Finally, seek out affordable options for entertainment and travel.

Take advantage of student discounts at museums, theaters, and other attractions. Explore free or low-cost activities like hiking, biking, or visiting local parks. Consider alternative lodging options like hostels or Airbnb for weekend getaways, and research travel deals and discounts to save money on transportation and accommodations.

Remember, financial independence is about making informed choices, prioritizing your spending, and finding creative ways to manage your finances. By budgeting wisely, exploring income opportunities, and seeking out affordable options, you can enjoy the freedom of off-campus exploration while also maintaining financial stability and avoiding unnecessary debt.

7.5 Building a Future: Exploring Career Options and Opportunities

College is not just about acquiring knowledge and earning a degree – it's also a stepping stone towards your future career and a chance to explore potential paths that align with your passions and aspirations. Your college town or city can be a valuable resource for exploring career options, gaining practical experience, and building connections in your chosen field.

Think of it as a launchpad for your professional journey, a chance to bridge the gap between academic theory and real-world application.

First, connect with your college's career center.

Career centers offer a wealth of resources, including career counseling, resume workshops, job fairs, and networking events. Take advantage of these services to explore potential career paths, develop your professional skills, and connect with potential employers.

Next, seek out internship opportunities.

Internships provide valuable hands-on experience in your field of interest, allowing you to apply your academic knowledge to real-world situations. Research local companies or organizations that align with your career goals and inquire about internship opportunities. Many colleges offer academic credit for internships, providing a win-win situation for both your academic and professional development.

Finally, network with professionals in your field.

Attend industry events, conferences, or workshops to connect with professionals in your chosen field. Utilize online networking platforms like LinkedIn to build connections and seek out mentorship opportunities. Networking can open doors to job opportunities, provide valuable insights into your industry, and help you build a professional network that will support your career growth.

Remember, your college experience is an investment in your future. By exploring career options, gaining practical experience through internships, and building professional connections, you'll lay the foundation for a successful and fulfilling career in your chosen field.

Conclusion:

Embracing the Journey, Shaping Your Future

As you stand on the precipice of your college experience, a mix of excitement and trepidation is completely natural. The transition from the familiar comforts of home to the uncharted territory of college life can feel like a thrilling roller coaster ride – exhilarating highs mixed with moments of doubt and uncertainty. Yet, within this journey lies a world brimming with possibilities, opportunities for personal growth and intellectual exploration, and the potential for forging lifelong connections that will shape your future.

This book has served as your guide, your compass navigating the vast and sometimes overwhelming landscape of college life. We've unpacked the practicalities of moving, from mastering the art of packing to transforming your dorm room into a cozy haven. We've delved into the intricacies of academic success, equipping you with strategies to navigate the academic system, crack the study code, and build relationships with professors who can become mentors and allies.

But college is more than just textbooks and exams. We've explored the vibrant tapestry of social life and campus culture, guiding you through the process of making friends, navigating the dating scene, and creating a sense of community within the larger college ecosystem. We've emphasized the importance of prioritizing your well-being, offering tools to manage stress and anxiety, build healthy relationships, and cultivate a positive mindset that will empower you to overcome challenges and thrive in the face of adversity.

Remember, there's no one-size-fits-all approach to the college experience. Each journey is unique, shaped by individual goals, aspirations, and the choices you make along the way. Embrace your own path, learn from the inevitable challenges, and celebrate your victories, big and small. Allow yourself to grow and evolve as you navigate this transformative chapter in your life.

College is a time for exploration, a chance to discover new passions, delve into uncharted intellectual territory, and connect with individuals from diverse backgrounds and perspectives. Step outside your comfort zone, embrace new experiences, and open yourself up to the transformative power of education, personal growth, and the bonds of friendship.

As you embark on this exciting adventure, remember that the lessons you learn, the challenges you overcome, and the memories you create will shape not only your college years but also the person you become. Cherish the moments, big and small, and allow yourself to be molded by the experiences that lie ahead. The future is yours to shape – go forth with confidence, embrace the journey, and conquer your dreams!

References:

Books:

The Naked Roommate: And 107 Other Issues You Might Run Into in College by Harlan Cohen

How to Win at College: Surprising Secrets for Success from the Country's Top Students by Cal Newport

The 7 Habits of Highly Effective College Students by Sean Covey

Conquering College: A Guide to Creating a Successful College Experience by Jonathan Morrow

Make It Stick: The Science of Successful Learning by Peter C. Brown, Henry L. Roediger III, and Mark A. McDaniel

Mindset: The New Psychology of Success by Carol S. Dweck

The Defining Decade: Why Your Twenties Matter–And How to Make the Most of Them Now by Meg Jay

Websites and Online Resources:

The National Survey of Student Engagement (NSSE): nsse.indiana.edu

The College Board: collegeboard.org

The Jed Foundation: jedfoundation.org (Focuses on emotional health and suicide prevention for teens and young adults)

Active Minds: activeminds.org (Student-run mental health advocacy group)

National Alliance on Mental Illness (NAMI): nami.org

The Trevor Project: thetrevorproject.org (Provides crisis intervention and suicide prevention services to LGBTQ youth)

Government Resources:

Federal Student Aid: studentaid.gov

Centers for Disease Control and Prevention (CDC): cdc.gov (Provides information on health and wellness topics relevant to college students)

Additional Resources:

College and university websites: Most colleges and universities have extensive resources available online for students, including information on academics, student life, housing, financial aid, and health and wellness services.

Campus newspapers and publications: These publications often provide insights into campus culture, events, and student perspectives.

Student organizations and clubs: Many student organizations have websites or social media pages that offer information on their activities and how to get involved.

Academic journals and publications: Explore academic journals related to your field of study for in-depth research and insights.

Online learning platforms: Platforms like Coursera, edX, and Khan Academy offer free or affordable online courses on a wide range of topics.

From Home to Halls: Conquering College Life with Confidence

College Bound? Navigate Your Move, Master Dorm Life, and Thrive on Campus!

Feeling a mix of excitement and overwhelm as you prepare for college? Worried about leaving home, making new friends, and succeeding academically? Unsure how to navigate the social scene and create a sense of belonging on campus?

As a recent college graduate who experienced the highs and lows of dorm life, academic challenges, and navigating the social scene, I understand the anxieties and uncertainties that come with transitioning to college. I've compiled my experiences, insights, and practical advice into this comprehensive guide to help you not just survive, but thrive during your college years.

Master the Move: Conquer packing, planning, and move-in day logistics with ease and efficiency.

Create Your Home Away from Home: Transform your dorm room into a cozy and personalized haven that reflects your style and inspires productivity.

Build a Supportive Network: Learn how to make friends, navigate roommate relationships, and build a sense of community on campus.

Unlock Academic Success: Discover effective study techniques, time management strategies, and tips for building relationships with professors.

Prioritize Your Well-Being: Develop healthy habits, manage stress, and cultivate a positive mindset for overall well-being.

Navigate the Social Scene: Explore campus culture, attend social events, and build lasting friendships with confidence.

Explore Beyond the Campus: Discover the hidden gems of your college town, plan exciting weekend adventures, and embrace new experiences.

Plan for Your Future: Explore career options, gain practical experience through internships, and build a professional network.

If you want to conquer college life with confidence, scroll up and buy this book today!

www.ingramcontent.com/pod-product-compliance
Lightning Source LLC
Chambersburg PA
CBHW070354230526
45471CB00006B/2566